Cooking Is Science

Katie Smythe

Rosen REAL READERS

Rosen Classroom™
New York

All About Grapes

Denzel T. Carter

Rosen REAL READERS

What is cooking? Cooking is how you make food. People have been cooking for a long time.

A cook makes food. There are cooks in restaurants. There are cooks at home. Do you know anyone who cooks?

A kitchen is where we cook food.
Kitchens have tools for cooking.

A pot is a cooking tool. Stoves are cooking tools as well. We find stoves in most kitchens. Stoves use heat. The heat cooks food.

We cook oatmeal on a stove. We cook soup on a stove. Can you think of other food cooked on a stove?

Let's make oatmeal. Ask an adult to help. You will need two parts milk and one part oats. This sounds like math!

How are the milk and the oats measured? Use a measuring cup. It is another cooking tool. We measure frequently in science!

Add two cups of milk to a pot. Heat the pot on a stove. Soon the milk will bubble.

Add one cup of oats to the hot milk. Stir the oats. It will be ready in a few minutes! Let it cool before eating. Fruit or honey will make it even more delicious!

Now you have used science to cook! You used math to measure the food. You used heat to cook the food. This science experiment is tasty!

Words to Know

cook

kitchen

oats

pot

stove

Rosen Real Readers
STEM AND STEAM TITLES

COOKING IS SCIENCE

For the Teacher
Science, technology, and math are subtly folded into the introduction of food, cooking, and kitchens. The end result is a fun recipe for children to try with their teachers. A picture-word glossary is included.

Text-Dependent Questions

1. Where do you cook food?
2. What cooking tools can you name?
3. How do you make oatmeal?

Open-Ended Questions

1. What cooking tools do you have in the kitchen?
2. What would you like to learn to cook?

Word Count: 219

Published in 2016 by the Rosen Publishing Group, Inc.
29 East 21st Street, New York, NY 10010

Book Design: Dean Galiano

Photo Credits: Cover and p. Saharosa40/iStock/Thinkstock; p. 2 DmitriyBezborodkin/iStock/Thinkstock; p. 3 TongRo Images /TongRo Images/Thinkstock; p. 4 Ryan McVay/Photosidc /Thinkstock; p. 5 Saharosa40/iStock/Thinkstock; p. 6 vonEisenstein /iStock/Thinkstock; p. 7 Wavebreakmedia Ltd/Wavebreakmedia /Thinkstock.

ISBN: 978-1-4994-9645-1
6-pack ISBN: 978-1-4994-9643-7

Manufactured in the United States of America

Rosen REAL READERS

Rosen Classroom™

ISBN-13: 978-1-4994-9781-6

9 781499 497816

E

ISBN: 978-1-4994-9781-6
6-pack ISBN: 978-1-4994-9779-3